# DELIBERATE DESPAIRS

## DESTINY IS WITHIN YOU

AJITHA.G

# Contents

# Preface

Success stories always begin with a bunch of failures. A part of describing ways to success ,this book also focuses on upholding it and making it ideal . All of our despairs are actually "Intentional" .They take shape because of our negligance. We might own a luxurious boat but what's it's purpose if we fail to row it and reach the bank safely? This book also motivates us to be a kind of ourselves who would differenciate between mind and soul and prioritize the soul which is the main entity of mankind.

# Acknowledgements

My first debth is to my professors who always motivate me to move forward with innovative ideas.Sincere thanks to my family,friends who encourage me to put forward my thoughts making them to reach millions of people all across the world.

# Prologue

This book consists of five chapters each describing a phase of the success.The content emphasises the need of self,efforts,contentment ,acceptance of surroundings and upholding the consistency to be ideal ,noble ,shine and prosper in all aspects.

CHAPTER ONE

# MIND VS SELF

THE INNER POTENTIAL OF THE HUMAN RACE IS WELL DEPICTED BY THE INNER SOUL.THE "SELFISH" MIND OFTEN DRIVES THE BODY TO SATISFY IT'S OWN NEEDS LEADING TO AN ERRONEOUS TRACK THAT PUTS THE MAN IN UNREST AND UNTOLERABLE STATE. THE URGE OF THE MIND IS WELL BALANCED BY THE SAGACIOUS SELF WHICH IS CAPABLE OF DISTINGUISHING AND INTERPRETING FOR SITUATIONS THAT ARE DILEMMATIC,PROBLEMETIC AND PREDICAMENT. SELF AND MIND ARE TWO DIFFERENT ENTITIES DEFINING THE STRUCTURE OF HUMAN CHARACTER. IN A RACE BETWEEN SELF AND MIND ,SELF SHOULD BE THE BREAD WINNER WINNING THE PREFERENCE AND CHOICE OF THE MAN. THE FOUNDATION OF THE SUCCESS IN EVERYONE'S LIFE BEGINS WITH THE RIGHT PURPOSE,RIGHT IDEAS AND RIGHT THOUGHTS THAT DRIVE THEM TO SEVERAL VISCOUS PATHS LEADING TO A CHARMING SUNSHINE OF VICTORY. SELF IS AN ENTITY WHICH REGULATES THE BODY'S WORKFLOW IN A RIGHT DIRECTION. THE CHOICES MADE BY A MAN ARE INDETERMINANT ,VAGUE AND INCONSISTENT.THE SELF IS WELL CAPABLE TO DISTINGUISH THE CHOICES AND MAKE A WISE DECISION.THE SELF IS RESPONSIBLE FOR THE OUTCOME OF EVERY ACTION AND THOUGHT. THE OUTCOME IS INDEED THE FORM OF VARIOUS PROCESSES UNDERGONE BY THE SELF IN CONFLICTING WITH THE MIND."MIND-BASED" ACTIONS ARE MOSTLY WORTHLESS WHEREAS "SELF-BASED"ACTIONS GET GLORY IN ONE'S LIFE. AN UNCONTROLLABLE MAN SEEMS TO BE UNHAPPY,DEPRIVED AND WORTHLESS.A MIND WELL CONTROLLED BY THE INNER SELF IS ALWAYS A SOURCE OF LIGHT WHICH IS ILLUMINATED TO ELIMINATE THE DARKNESS IN THE MAN KIND. IT GLORIFIES THE

HUMAN SPIRIT WITH AN UNKNOWN ENERGY TAKING IT'S SHAPE WHILE TRANSFORMING INTO OTHER.THIS ENERGY HOLDS THE MANKIND WITH A FORCE DESTROYING THE EVIL-MINDED AND MALEVOLENT THOUGHTS RESPONSIBLE FOR THE DESTRUCTION OF THE UNIVERSE.A TRUE SELF BINDS THE WORLD BY UNITING THE BROKEN FRAGMENTS DEFINING THE POWER OF ITSELF. IT DEFINES THE TRUE MEANING OF MANKIND.A FIRM FOUNDATION FOR MANKIND CAN BE LAID ONLY WHEN MIND AND SOUL ARE WELL DISTINGUISHED.

CHAPTER TWO

# EFFORTS AND THEIR OUTCOMES

AFTER REALISING THE DIFFERENCE BETWEEN MIND AND SELF,YOU ARE NOW IN A POSITION TO DESIRE ,DESIGN THE METHEDOLOGIES AND ASPIRE FOR IMPACTFUL-TRANSFORMATION WITHIN YOURSELF. IS IT SUFFICIENT IF YOU JUST ASPIRE FOR A CAUSE? DON'T YOU REQUIRE IT'S RESULT?HOW DO YOU EXPERIENCE THE TASTE OF YOUR IDEAS WITHOUT PUTTING EFFORTS?HOW WOULD APPLES BE SWEET WITHOUT RIPENING?YOUR BODY IS AN INSTRUMENT OF YOUR INNER SELF. IF "SELF" HAS THE ABILITY TO SOW THE SEEDS OF ASPIRATIONS WITHIN YOU,IT EVEN HAS THE ABILITY TO CULTIVATE THE CROPS OF SUCCESS. THIS REQUIRES HUMAN LABOUR,SWEAT AND WORK. OUR MIND LOOKS FOR IT'S COMFORT ZONE. THIS ZONE IS AS HAZARDOUS AS A POISON . A MAN EMBODIED IN THIS ZONE CAN NEVER GET UP TO ACQUIRE AND UNLEASH HIS HIDDEN TALENTS.OUR SELFV IS THE PRIMARY ENTITY WHICH DRIVES OUR BODY TO SWEAT,WORK AND TOIL TO FULFILL ASPIRATIONS.IT'S IN THE DECISION OF THE MIND TO EXECUTE THE IKDEAS IN THE FORM OF LABOUR.THE OUTCOME OF THE EFFORT MAY OR MAY NOT BE POSITIVE. THIS CLASSIFICATION CAN BE CONSIDERED INTO TWO PARTS

1)POSITIVE EFFORT - POSITIVE RESULT
2) POSITIVE EFFORT - NEGATIVE RESULT
3)NEGATIVE EFFORT - POSITIVE RESULT
4)NEGATIVE EFFORT - NEGATIVE RESULT

## ***EFFORT VS RESULT MODEL***

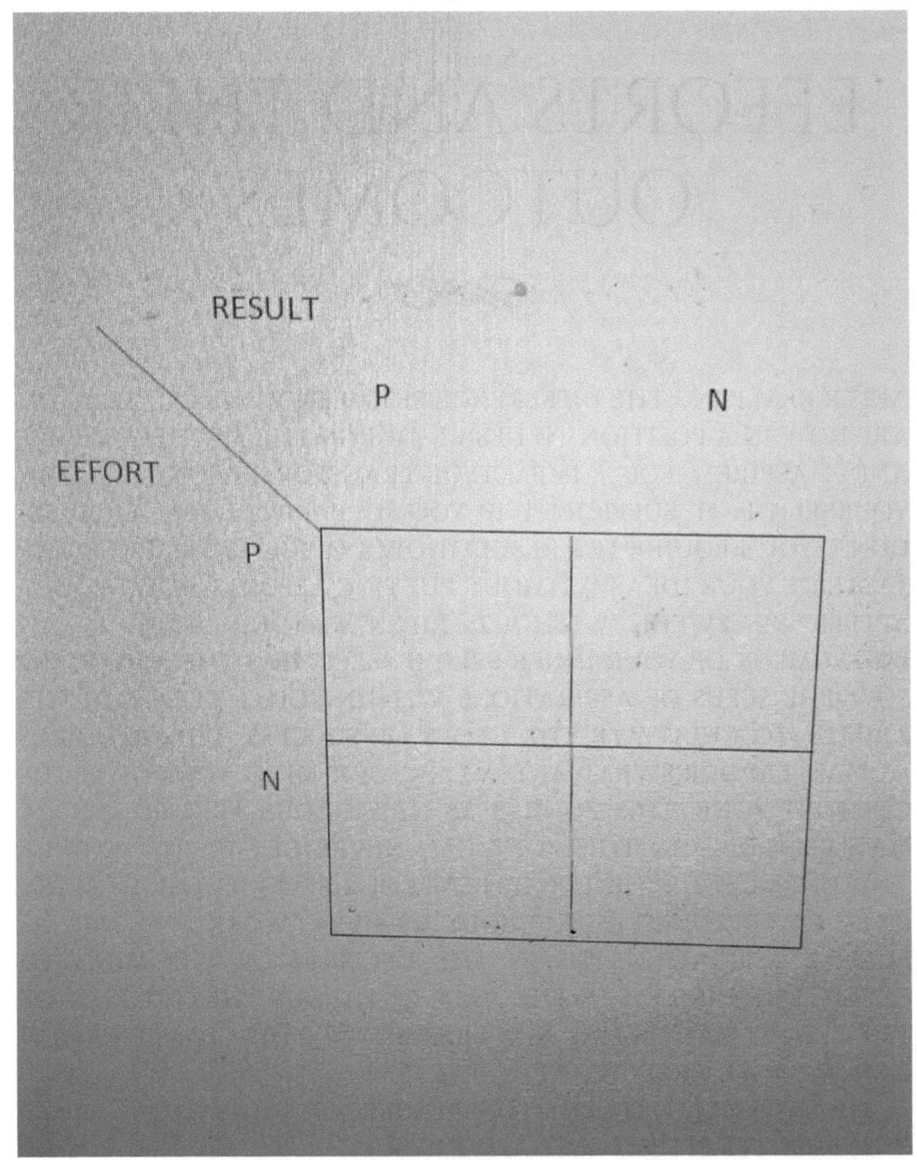


P-Positive , N-Negative

FOR EXAMPLE,IF WE ENCOUNTER POSITIVE RESULT FOR OUR FULL EFFORTS(POSITIVE EFFORTS) WE THEN ALLOT "1" CORRESPONDING TO POSITIVE EFFORT-POSITIVE RESULT (P-P 1) .THEN, EFFORT VS RESULT MODEL WOULD BE

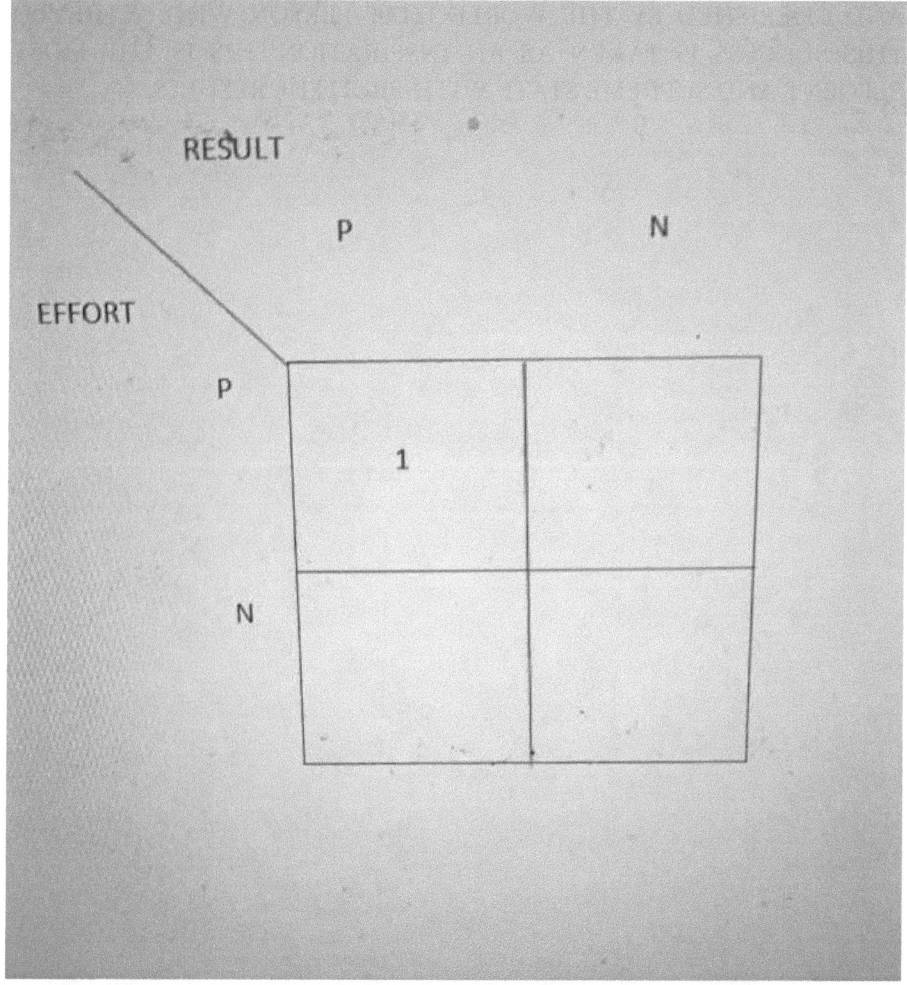


THE SAME IS APPLIED TO REST ALL CASES OF EFFORTS AND THEIR CORRESPONDING RESULTS.

•

## POSITIVE EFFORTS -POSITIVE RESULT(P-P 1)

THIS IS AN ABSOLUTE DESIRED AND ASPIRED STATE OF A MAN. OBTAINING THE DESIRED RESULTS FOR FULL EFFORTS DEFINES THE SUCCESS IN ATRUE SENSE. THIS KIND OF SUCCESS IS REMEMBERED AND CHERISHED BY THE WORLD.THAT PERSON WHO ACHIEVED THIS SUCCESS IS TAKEN AS AN INSPIRATION.THIS IS THE MOST ELEGENT AND SUPREME STATE WITH FRUITFUL RESULTS.

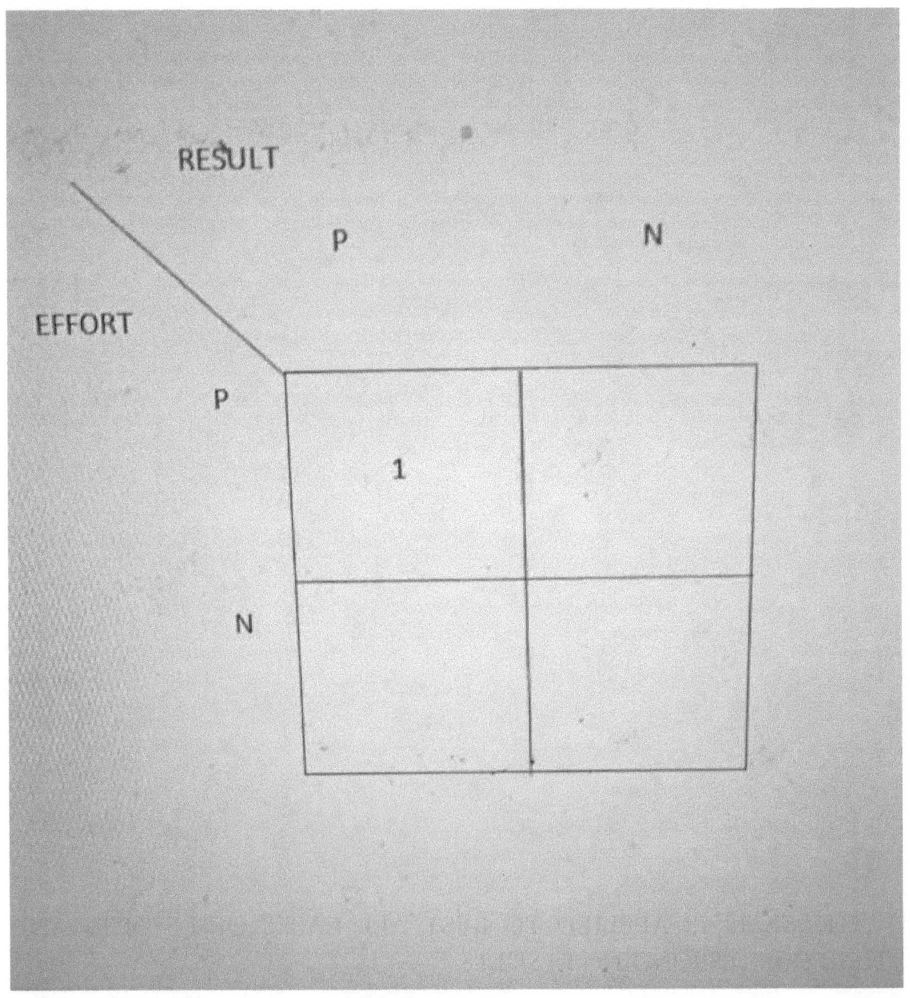

•

## POSITIVE EFFORTS-NEGATIVE RESULT(P-N 1)

THIS PHASE IS PERHAPS THE FOUNDATION OF MANY SUCCESSFUL SCIENTISTS,ARTISTS AND MANY OTHER NOBLE MEN.OBTAINING UNDESIRED OUTCOMES FOR COMPLETE EFFORTS CAN NEVER BE DEFINED AS FAILURE. IN FACT,IT JUST DEMANDS FOR THE BETTER METHEDOLOGIES IN WHICH ONE CAN WORK TO IMPROVE THE THROUGHPUT AND QUALITY OF THE OUTCOME.IT JUDGES AND EVALUATES THE UNRIGHTEOUS PATHS UNDERTAKEN AND MAKES US NOBLE,EFFICIENT AND SELF-REALIZABLE.GIVING UP UNDER THESE CIRCUMSTANCES INDICATES ONE'S ABILITY OF GETTING DEMORALIZED AND AGITATED.EVERY NOBLE PERSOM WALKING IN AN IDEAL PATH MUST PASS THROUGH THE FOREST OF IMPEDIMENTS WHICH ULTIMATELY LEADS TO A SUN-SHINE.BY GETTING UP FROM THE HURDLES,YOU CAN CONVERT THE NEGATIVE UNDESIRABLE OUTCOMES INTO POSITIVE DESIRABLE DESTINATION WHICH ULTIMATELY DEFINES SUCCESS.

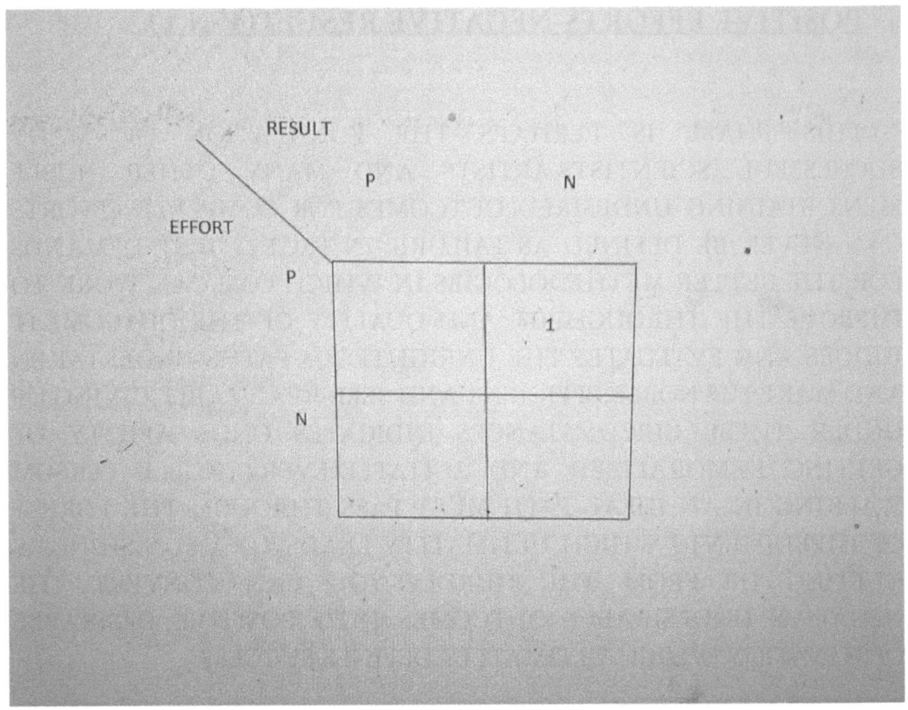


- 

## NEGATIVE EFFORTS-NEGATIVE RESULT (N-N 1)

IT IS AN ULTIMATE AND NATURAL PHENOMINA OF OBTAINING UNDESIRABLE OUTCOME FOR ZERO EFFORTS.ASPIRING FOR A GREAT TRANSFORMATION ITSELF ISN'T ENOUGH FOR A BETTER MANKIND.LABOUR DEFINES THE WILL POWER AND FULFILLS YOUR QUEST FOR HAPPINESS.YOU'D STEP AHEAD TO DRILL YOUR BODY IF YOUR ASPIRATIONS ARE STRONG AND WORTHY.YOU'D EXPERIENCE THE FRUITS ONLY WHEN YOU TOIL,COLLAPSE,FAIL AND GET UP.EVERY ATTEMPT HAS IT'S OUTCOME WHICH DEFINES YOU IN VARIOUS WAYS.

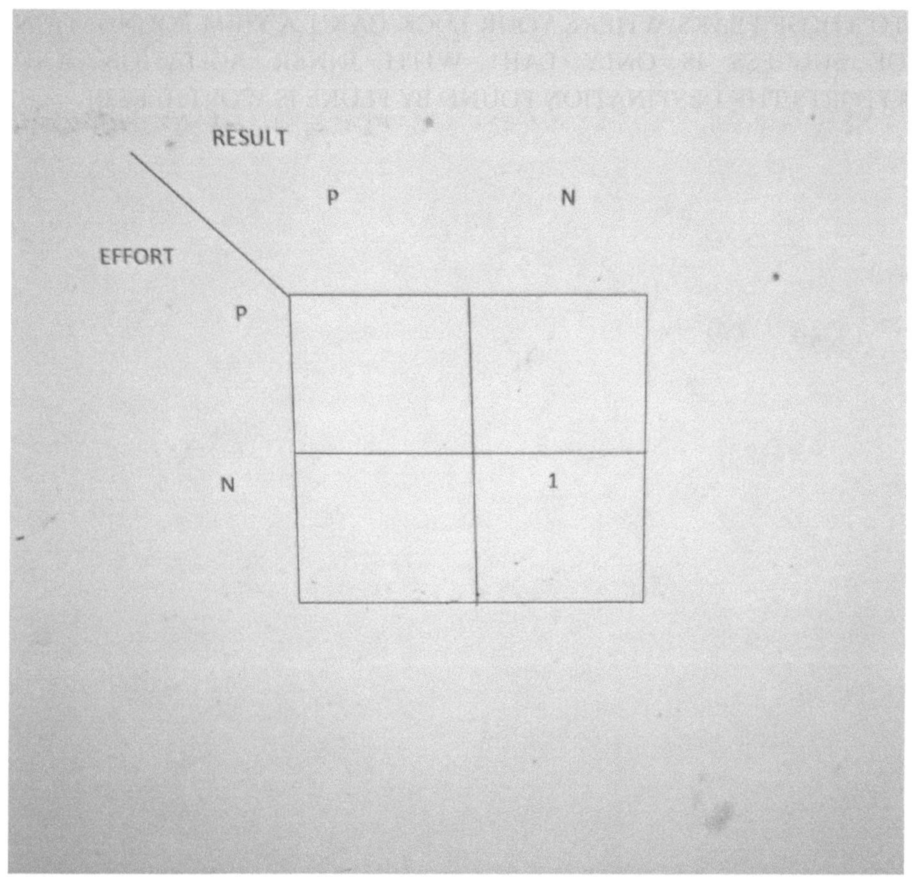


- **NEGATIVE EFFORT-POSITIVE RESULT(N-P 1)**

THIS IS ENCOUNTERED WHEN YOUR LUCK KNOCKS YOUR DOOR.PERHAPS,THAT ISN'T A LONG LASTING SUCCESS. IT MIGHT PUT YOU IN A STATE OF TURMOIL.A THIEF CAN BE JAMMY ENOUGH TO FIND TREASURE UNDERGROUND BUT MAY NOT BE CAPABLE ENOUGH TO UPHOLD IT FOR A LONGER TIME.YOU'D ENJOY THIS KIND OF SUCCESS ONLY IF YOUR FATE MEANS TO UPHOLD IT.IN MOST OF THE CASES,THIS JOY IS TEMPORARY AND IMMEDIATLY

TAKEN AWAY BY YOUR DESTINY.YOUR HARDWORK CAN TAKE YOU TO THOSE PEAKS WHERE YOUR LUCK CAN'T.A FIRM FOUNDATION OF SUCCESS IS ONLY LAID WITH INNER AGITATION AND EFFORTS.THE DESTINATION FOUND BY FLUKE IS WORTHLESS!!

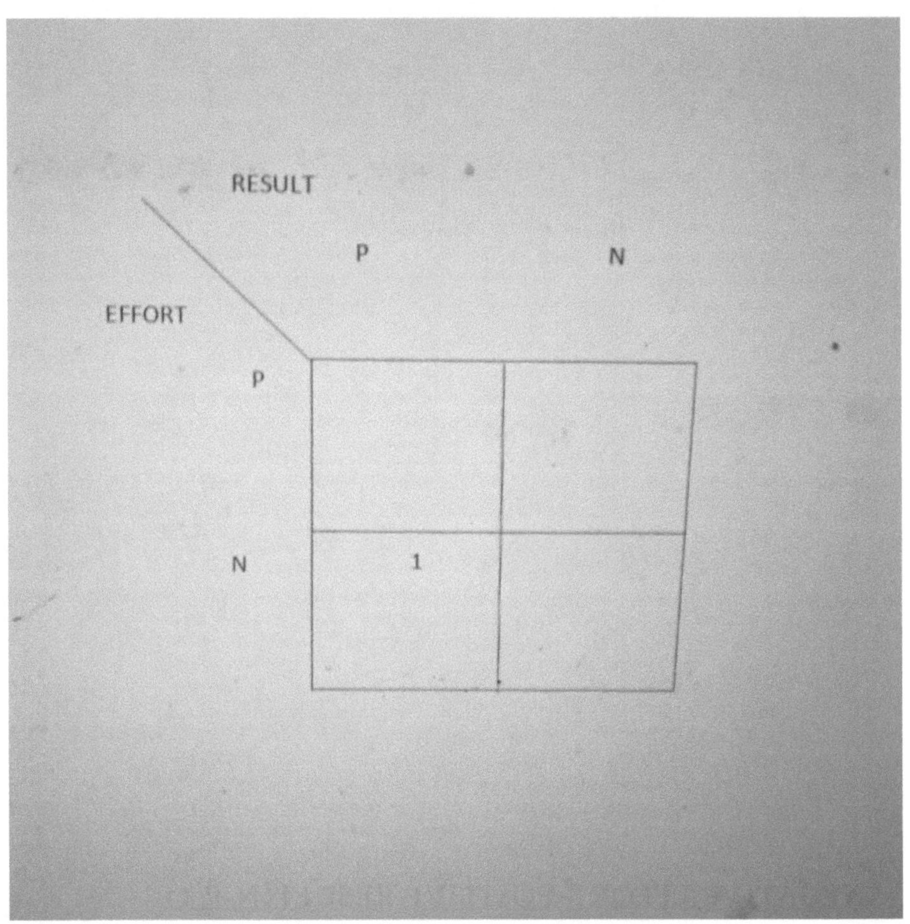

CHAPTER THREE

# CONTENTMENT

AN EMPLOYEE OF A COMPANY SAYS "WELL,I"VE EARNED 1 LAKH .I AM NOW IN A POSITION TO FULFILL MY BASIC REQUIREMENTS AND SUPPORT MY FAMILY FINANCIALLY.I SHOULD NOW BE ABLE TO BALANCE MY PERSONAL AND PROFESSIONAL RESPONSIBILITIES".A BUSINESS TYCOON SAYS"WE'VE MADE A GOOD PROFIT THIS YEAR.THIS IS AN UNFORGETTABLE ACHIEVEMENT.LET'S EARN MORE AND MORE.LETS DRILL OUR EMPLOYEES MORE AND TRIPLE OUR PROFIT" FROM THIS ANALOGY AND VIEWS OF TWO DIFFERENT PROFESSIONAL MINDSETS ,WE CAN CONFER THAT THE LATTER ONE HAS A LACK OF CONTENTMENT WITHIN SELF.IN A BROADER SENSE,OUR SELF IS NOURISHED BY CONTENTMENT. THE MORE IS THE CONTENTMENT ,THE GREATER WILL BE THE INNER HAPPINESS. YOU MIGHT NOT BE ABLE TO BUILD A WAY TO HEAVEN. APPRECIATE THE FACT THAT YOU MADE A WAY WHICH CLEARED YOUR YESTERDAY'S DESPAIRS AND DESPONDENTS.YOUR SELF-SATISFACTION MAKES YOU GROW PEACEFULLY WITHOUT EXTERNAL AND INTERNAL PRESSURES.EUPHONY GETS ESTABLISHED BETWEEN MIND AND SELF BY CALMING DOWN THE UNWANTED -DEVELOPING DESIRES WITHIN YOU. YOU'D LOOSE THE HARD-EARNED "MINIMUM" YOU HAVE IF YOU DESIRE MORE THAN "MAXIMUM".BE HAPPY WITH WHAT YOU HAVE AT PRESENT AND PROSPER PEACEFULLY.

CHAPTER FOUR

# THE ENVIOUS NEIGHBOURHOOD.

EMBRACE THE FACT THAT NOT ALL WILL BE THE POSITIVE ACCEPTORS OF YOUR SUCCESS.ADMIT THE FACT THAT YOU'D FACE CRITICISM BY THE PUBLIC AFTER ESTABLISHING YOUR SUCCESS BEFORE THEM.THEY TRY TO DRENCH YOU,THEY DEMOTIVATE YOU,THEY WRONG YOU AND FINALLY THEY START HATING YOU.NEVER FALL IN THE TRAP OF WRONG MEN.NEVER LET YOURSELF DOWN IF THEY DRENCH YOU. YOU SHOULD'NT STOP YOUR VOYAGE IN MIDDLE OF THE SEA EVEN THOUGH YOUR SHIP IS SURROUNDED BY VIOLENT SHARKS.YOU MUST BE ABLE TO PASS THROUGH THE ADHESIVE AND TENACIOUS WAY CONSISTING OF CROOKS AND VICTIMIZERS.PEOPLE GATHER TO PROVE YOU WRONG.YOU SHOULD GET UP AND GATHER YOUR THESIS AND HYPOTHESIS TO PROVE YOURSELVES. OUR OWN FRIENDS MIGHT TURN AS FOES.OUR WELL-WISHERS MIGHT TURN ILL-MANNERED AND RIVAL .YOU'LL THEN UNDERSTAND THE CHANGING COLOURS OF THE WORLD. OUR NEIGHBOURHOOD WILL NEVER REMAIN CONSISTENT.FEW PAMPER YOU TO THE SKY AND FEW DEMOTIVATE YOU.YOUR SUCCESS ITSELF CAN GET YOU LOT MANY CHALLENGES AND SURPRISES.YOUR SUCCESS CAN BE YOUR BEST FRIEND AS WELL AS YOUR FOE.NEVER GIVE UP OR SACRIFICE YOUR SUCCESS FOR THE SAKE OF SOMEONE.YOUR ABILITY LIES IN FILTERING OUT UNWANTED ENTITIES BROUGHT BY YOUR SUCCESS AND ENJOY THE FRUITS BROUGHT BY IT.

CHAPTER FIVE

# RETAIN YOUR CONGRUITY

UPHOLDING THE CONSISTENCY OF YOUR EFFORTS IS ANOTHER KEY FACTOR TO MEASURE YOUR SUCCESS.DO YOU EVER WILL TO BE PAID ONLY FOR A MONTH?EVERY WORKER SHOULD MAKE OUT FOR ONE WHOLE LIFETIME TO EARN THE LIVING.SUCCESS CAN'T BE ONCE IN A LIFETIME.SUCCESS IS A JOUNEYWHICH ALSO MEANS THE EVER-LASTING FLOW OF SWEAT.YOU SHOULD'NT SIT QUIET ONCE YOUR DESTINATION IS REACHED.YOU MUST BE ABLE TO PRODUCE THE SIMILAR KIND OF PERSISTENCE,DETERMINATION AND PRESERVERANCE TO MAINTAIN THAT SUCCESS RATE THROUGHOUT YOUR LIFE.UPHOLDING YOUR SUCCESS MATTERS WHEN YOU WISH TO PROVE YOURSELVES TO THE DISAGREEABLE SOCIETY.IT ALSO MATTERS WHEN YOU WISH TO STAND BY YOURSELVES AND WHEN THE WHOLE WORLD STANDS AGAINST YOUR ACHIEVEMENTS.THE MOST HILARIOUS THING IS WHEN PEOPLE ASSUME THAT YOUR SUCCESS IS JUST A FLUKE.PEOPLE WOULD NEVER QUESTION YOUR SUCCESS IF YOUR SWEAT FLOWS THROUGHOUT YOUR LIFE AND PRODUCE THE FRUITS THAT BEAR THE TASTE OF YOUR VICTORY.

YOU CANNOT HIT THE JACKPOT WITHOUT AMALGAMATION OF SELF,LABOUR,CONTENTMENT,ACCEPTANCE AND CONSISTENCY. EVERY SHINING STAR IS A RESULT OF BURNING AND TOILING. EVERY DAY COMES WITH A MESSAGE OF BEGINING A NEW PHASE OF LIFE WHICH ERASES OUR GRIEF-STICKEN PAST AND PAVES A WAY TO CHEERFUL FUTURE FILLED WITH SHIMMER AND SHINE.

Printed by Libri Plureos GmbH in Hamburg,
Germany